Dealing with Challenges

Family Changes

By Meg Gaertner

level
2
little blue
readers

www.littlebluehousebooks.com

Little Blue House is distributed by North Star Editions:
sales@northstareditions.com | 888-417-0195

Produced for Little Blue House by Red Line Editorial.

Photographs ©: Shutterstock Images, cover, 4, 6, 8–9, 12–13, 16, 19 (top), 19 (bottom), 20–21, 24 (top left), 24 (top right), 24 (bottom left), 24 (bottom right); iStockphoto, 11, 15, 23

Library of Congress Control Number: 2021916803

ISBN
978-1-64619-484-1 (hardcover)
978-1-64619-511-4 (paperback)
978-1-64619-563-3 (ebook pdf)
978-1-64619-538-1 (hosted ebook)

Printed in the United States of America
Mankato, MN
012022

About the Author

Meg Gaertner enjoys reading, writing, dancing, and being outside. She lives in Minnesota.

Table of Contents

Family Changes

Sometimes families change.

A family member may go away, or a new member may be added.

These changes can be hard.

Kinds of Changes

Sometimes parents no longer want to be married.

They decide they would be happier apart.

They get a divorce.

The parents are no

longer married.

They live in different places.

This is not an easy decision, and

it is not the child's fault.

Sometimes a parent marries someone new.

This new person is the child's stepparent.

This person may have children.

They are the child's stepbrothers or stepsisters.

stepmother

father

The child's mom might have
a baby.
This baby will be a new brother
or sister.
A new baby brings
many changes.

Parents or family members
might have to go away.
This can happen for
many reasons.
Sometimes the child can visit,
and sometimes the child cannot.

Getting Help

Change is a part of life.

But it takes time to get used to change.

You might miss how things

were before.

Maybe you feel sad or alone.

Or maybe you aren't sure how you feel.

Exercise can help you let out your feelings.

Drawing pictures can help, too.

Ask for a family meeting.

Share how you feel, and

ask questions.

Listen to others' feelings, too.

These changes are new

for everyone.

Things may be different now.

But your family still loves you.

Their love for you has
not changed.

Glossary

baby

family meeting

exercise

picture

Index